Yusra Mardini
Refugee Hero and Olympic Swimmer

Kelly Spence

Crabtree Publishing Company
www.crabtreebooks.com

Author: Kelly Spence

Series research and development: Reagan Miller

Editorial director: Kathy Middleton

Editor: Ellen Rodger

Proofreader: Wendy Scavuzzo

Photo researcher: Samara Parent

Designer and prepress technician: Samara Parent

Print coordinator: Katherine Berti

Library and Archives Canada Cataloguing in Publication

Spence, Kelly, author
    Yusra Mardini : refugee hero and Olympic swimmer / Kelly Spence.

(Remarkable lives revealed)
Includes index.
Issued in print and electronic formats.
ISBN 978-0-7787-4711-6 (hardcover).--
ISBN 978-0-7787-4726-0 (softcover).--ISBN 978-1-4271-2079-3 (HTML)

    1. Mardini, Yusra--Juvenile literature. 2. Women swimmers--Syria--Biography--Juvenile literature. 3. Swimmers--Syria--Biography--Juvenile literature. 4. Women Olympic athletes--Syria--Biography--Juvenile literature. 5. Olympic athletes--Syria--Biography--Juvenile literature. 6. Women refugees--Syria--Biography--Juvenile literature. 7. Refugees--Syria--Biography--Juvenile literature. 8. Women social reformers--Syria--Biography--Juvenile literature. 9. Social reformers--Syria--Biography--Juvenile literature. I. Title. II. Series: Remarkable lives revealed

GV838.M33S64 2018   j797.2'1092   C2017-907730-9
                                                 C2017-907731-7

Library of Congress Cataloging-in-Publication Data

Names: Spence, Kelly, author.
Title: Yusra Mardini : refugee hero and Olympic swimmer / Kelly Spence
Description: New York : Crabtree Publishing Company, [2018] | Series: Remarkable Lives Revealed | Includes index.
Identifiers: LCCN 2017057538 (print) | LCCN 2018003262 (ebook) | ISBN 9781427120793 (Electronic HTML) | ISBN 9780778747116 (Reinforced library binding : alk. paper) | ISBN 9780778747260 (Paperback : alk. paper)
Subjects: LCSH: Mardini, Yusra,--Juvenile literature. | Swimmers--Biography--Juvenile literature. | Olympic Games (31st : 2016 : Rio de Janeiro, Brazil)--History--Juvenile literature. | Women swimmers--Biography--Juvenile literature.
Classification: LCC GV838.M366 (ebook) | LCC GV838.M366 S64 2018 (print) | DDC 797.2/1092 [B] --dc23
LC record available at https://lccn.loc.gov/2017057538

Crabtree Publishing Company

www.crabtreebooks.com   1-800-387-7650

Printed in the U.S.A./032018/BG20180202

Published in Canada
Crabtree Publishing
616 Welland Ave.
St. Catharines, Ontario
L2M 5V6

Published in the United States
Crabtree Publishing
PMB 59051
350 Fifth Ave., 59th Floor
New York, NY 10118

Published in the United Kingdom
Crabtree Publishing
Maritime House
Basin Road North, Hove
BN41 1WR

Published in Australia
Crabtree Publishing
3 Charles Street
Coburg North
VIC, 3058

Contents

Introduction Stories of Survival......................4

Chapter 1 Growing Up in Syria 6

Chapter 2 Escaping to Europe 10

Chapter 3 Team Refugee 18

Chapter 4 Standing Together 24

Writing Prompts 30

Learning More....................................31

Glossary 32

Index 32

Stories of Survival

There are many different kinds of stories. Some stories are about survival, such as fleeing from war. Others are about chasing dreams. In 2015, Yusra Mardini (YOOS-rah MAR-deen-ee) was only 17 years old when she fled her home in war-torn Syria (SEER-ee-uh). She became famous after she helped rescue a boat full of people as it was sinking in the sea. Less than a year later, she competed at the Summer Olympics in Brazil.

What Is a Biography?

A **biography** is the story of a person's experiences. We read biographies to learn about another person's life. A biography can be based on many sources of information. Primary sources include a person's own words or pictures. Secondary sources include friends, family, media, and research.

*By sharing her story, Yusra has helped raise awareness about the global refugee **crisis**.*

Becoming a Refugee

Yusra became a **refugee** when she left Syria. A refugee is a person who flees from his or her country. They leave for many reasons. Some refugees escape war. Others leave because they are being **persecuted**, or because of a **natural disaster**, such as an earthquake. By June 2017, there were more than 22.5 million refugees around the world.

? THINK ABOUT IT

Yusra's story has inspired many people. As you read this book, think about the special traits that make this young woman so remarkable.

Growing Up in Syria

Yusra's journey began in her home country of Syria. She was born on March 5, 1998, in the capital city of Damascus (duh-MAS-kuhs). Growing up, Yusra had a safe and happy childhood. Her father Ezzat (EZZ-zat) was a swimming coach. Her mother Mervat (MEER-vat) worked as a **physiotherapist**. Yusra was their second daughter. Her big sister Sarah was three when Yusra was born. Their little sister Shahed (SHAA-hed) was born 11 years later.

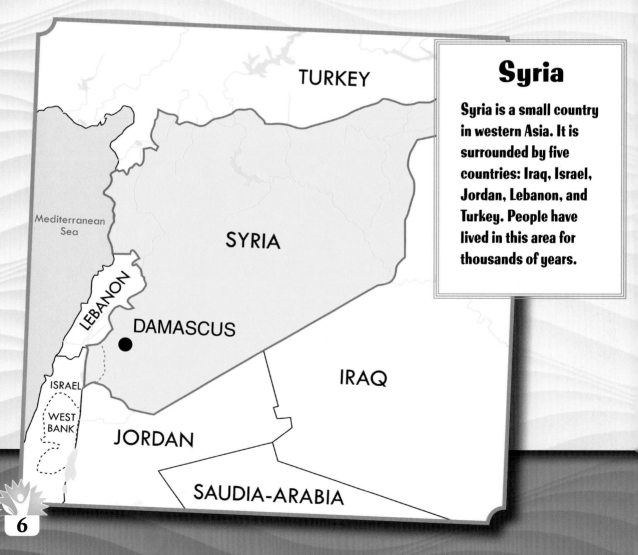

Syria

Syria is a small country in western Asia. It is surrounded by five countries: Iraq, Israel, Jordan, Lebanon, and Turkey. People have lived in this area for thousands of years.

At Home in the Water

Yusra began swimming when she was three. As she grew up, she started to compete in races. Family life centered around the pool. Yusra's father coached his talented daughters. Sometimes the girls would train for up to nine hours a day. All their hard work paid off, and soon the sisters earned spots on the Syrian national team.

Yusra dreamed about going to the Olympics. She admired American swimmer Michael Phelps and Jamaican sprinter Usain (YOO-sane) Bolt.

> "
> _When I was a little kid, I was just put into the water._
>
> —**Yusra Mardini,** _New York Times_ **interview, 2016**
> "

War Begins

In March 2011, many Syrians began **protesting** against their government. They marched in the streets fighting for **democracy**. The protestors wanted to vote for a new government and have more freedom. But the government refused to give up power and attacked the protestors. Soon a **civil war** erupted between the Syrian government and **rebel** groups. At first, Yusra's life was not greatly affected by the war. That changed in 2012. That year, the fighting reached the neighborhood where the Mardinis lived.

Women from Damascus carry banners that plead for an end to the war that has killed more than 480,000 people.

Danger in Damascus

Hundreds of people were killed and buildings were destroyed. The family moved to a safer area. In December, Yusra competed at the world championships in Turkey. But soon it became too dangerous to keep swimming. A bomb tore the roof off the pool where she trained. Two of her teammates were killed. Yusra's father left Syria to live in Jordan where he could work and send money home to his family.

Homes, schools, and businesses are left in ruins after years of fighting. The Syrian Civil War has forced half of the country's population, or 11 million people, to flee to safer parts of Syria or other countries.

> *Once I was like you. I had a home, I had roots, I belonged. Like you, I lived my life day-to-day, caught up in my hopes, passions, and problems. Then war came and everything changed.*
>
> **—Yusra Mardini, World Economic Forum speech, 2017**

Escaping to Europe

Yusra and Sarah missed swimming and the life they had before the war. They saw no future in Syria. By August 2015, they decided to go to Germany where they could continue training. Their father allowed them to go to Turkey along with two male relatives. From there, they crossed the Mediterranean (Med-it-tuh-REY-nee-uhn) Sea to reach Europe. Their mother and younger sister followed later.

These Syrians were captured by the Turkish Coast Guard while trying to flee to Greece.

The Journey to the Coast

The sisters flew from Syria to Lebanon (LEB-uh-nuhn). Then another plane took them to Turkey. In Turkey, they boarded a bus to the coast. Greece lay across the sea. The group met with a smuggler. Smugglers move people or items **illegally** from one country to another. They paid the smuggler $1,200 U.S. to bring them across the water to Greece.

THINK ABOUT IT

Why do you think some countries welcome refugees, while others do not?

Refugee Crisis

More than 1 million people fled war and conflict in the Middle East, Asia, and Africa in 2015. Most went to Europe. The influx of so many people caused a crisis for many countries. Refugees need food, water, and shelter. Some countries tried to close their **borders**. Others welcomed them.

Across the Water

Before they could leave the shores of Turkey, the sisters waited in the woods for four days. During their first attempt to cross the water, the Turkish police forced their boat to turn back. On the next trip, more than 20 people were crammed onto a rubber boat meant to hold about 7 people. The journey lasted about an hour and a half.

In 2015, more than 300,000 refugees crossed the Mediterranean Sea.

Sink or Swim

Fifteen minutes after leaving shore, the boat's motor died. The crowded boat was swamped and in danger of **capsizing**. Only a few people onboard knew how to swim. Sarah and Yusra bravely plunged into the sea. Two men followed. Together, they grabbed hold of the boat and began towing it toward shore. Sarah's soaked clothing was dragging her down. A passenger cut material off her pants so they would be lighter. As she kicked, Yusra lost her shoes. Exhausted yet determined, they pushed on through the cold, dark water.

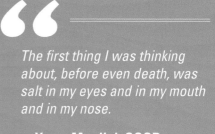

> The first thing I was thinking about, before even death, was salt in my eyes and in my mouth and in my nose.
>
> —Yusra Mardini, GOOD interview, September 2017

To lighten the load on the small boat, luggage was thrown overboard. The shores of the Greek islands were strewn with clothing and toys left behind by refugees.

Safety on Shore

After three-and-a-half hours at sea, the boat reached shore at dawn. Everyone had survived the crossing. The refugees landed on the Island of Lesbos. Exhausted, Sarah and Yusra phoned their father to tell him they were alive. Even after the dangerous journey, many challenges lay ahead. In many countries, refugees are not welcomed. On Lesbos, businesses refused to sell the sisters food and water. But there were people who offered help, too. Along the road, a kind stranger gave Yusra a pair of shoes to replace the ones she had lost in the sea.

? THINK ABOUT IT

How do you think small acts of kindness, such as being given a pair of shoes, affected Yusra? Why?

The Journey on Land

From Lesbos, the sisters boarded a boat to the mainland. They then walked on foot and rode on trains and buses through Macedonia (mas-i-DOH-nee-uh) and Serbia (SUR-bee-uh). At the border between Serbia and Hungary, they hid from the police in a cornfield. They were stopped at a train station, then taken to a refugee camp. A few days later, the girls left the camp and continued traveling north through Austria. After 25 days, they reached Germany in September 2015.

> None of us could have prepared for that journey. The desperate prayers at sea, the long trek, the humiliation at the barbed wire. But however hard it was, we knew there was no way back. We'd already lost everything, there was no choice but to keep running, for shelter, for peace.
>
> —**Yusra Mardini at the World Economic Forum, January 2017**

A boat full of refugees lands on Lesbos Island.

A New Home in Germany

In Germany, the sisters settled in the capital, Berlin. They lived there in a refugee camp for six months. Each day, Yusra and Sarah lined up for hours to receive **asylum** papers from the German government. They worked hard to learn the language and to build a life in their new home.

Granting Asylum

There are different words used to describe a person who flees their homeland. When they arrive in another country, they are called an asylum-seeker. After the person is granted asylum, they can legally stay in the country. They are then called a refugee.

? THINK ABOUT IT

Imagine that you suddenly had to move to a new country. How would you feel? What challenges might you face?

In Berlin, Yusra studied hard to learn German.

Back in the Water

Yusra and Sarah met a **translator** at the camp. He helped them find a local swimming club. At the club, they met a coach named Sven (s-VEHN). The girls were soon back in the water training twice a day. Unfortunately, Sarah then learned she could no longer compete. While towing the boat across the sea, she had aggravated an old shoulder injury. But Sven could see that Yusra had talent. With hard work and determination, he believed his new swimmer had the potential to make her Olympic dream come true.

> " When my sister wants to encourage me she says: show them what a refugee can do.
>
> —Yusra Mardini, *Telegraph*, August 7, 2016 "

Team Refugee

By early 2016, Yusra and Sarah had left the refugee camp and moved into their own apartment. The family was reunited when her parents and younger sister arrived in Berlin. Sarah and Yusra had been granted asylum, and this made it easier for their family to come to Germany. While the family was happy to be together, they worried about their friends and family trapped in Syria.

> "
>
> *I want to represent all the refugees because I want to show everyone that, after the pain, after the storm, comes calm days. I want to inspire them to do something good in their lives.*
>
> — **Yusra in an interview with *Teen Vogue*, March 28, 2016**
>
> "

Yusra trains at a pool that was built for the 1936 Olympics, which took place in Berlin.

The Road to Rio

In the pool, Yusra was focused on getting faster and stronger. Her goal was to compete at the 2020 Olympics in Tokyo, Japan. That changed in March. The International Olympic Committee (IOC) announced that a team of refugees would compete at the 2016 Games in Rio de Janeiro (REE-oh dey zhuh-NAIR-oh), Brazil. Yusra's coach thought she had a good chance to make the team. Forty-three athletes applied, only ten were selected. Yusra was chosen and given a **scholarship** to help her train. While most athletes spend years preparing for the Olympics, Yusra had to be ready in just a few months.

Under the Olympic Flag

Team Refugee was made up of ten athletes from Syria, South Sudan, the Democratic Republic of the Congo, and Ethiopia. They would compete in three sports: swimming, running, and **judo**. No one represented their home country. Instead, the athletes would compete under the Olympic flag.

The Olympic Flag

The Olympic flag has five rings in six different colors that represents the colors used on flags all over the world. By allowing Team Refugee to use its flag, the Olympics showed its support for the millions of refugees around the world.

Yusra marches with fellow Team Refugee members at the opening ceremony of the games.

The Games Begin

On August 5, the opening ceremonies marked the beginning of the 2016 Rio Olympics. Yusra and her teammates marched into the stadium alongside athletes from more than 200 countries. Team Refugee entered ahead of Brazil, the host country. Everyone stood and cheered. It was the first time a team of refugees competed at the Games.

> " These refugees have no home, no team, no flag, no national anthem. We will offer them a home in the Olympic Village, together with all the athletes of the world. The Olympic anthem will be played in their honor, and the Olympic flag will lead them into the Olympic Stadium.
>
> —**Thomas Bach, president of the IOC** "

Before the Games began, Yusra and her teammates visited Christ the Redeemer, a statue that overlooks Rio.

On the Olympic Stage

Yusra's first Olympic race was the women's 100-meter butterfly, which is her favorite stroke. Her family was in the stands to cheer her on. She won her **heat**, but did not qualify for the next race. Her second event was the 100-meter freestyle. Yusra did not qualify for the next race, ending her competition in Rio. Although she did not leave with a medal, her Olympic experience was about more than winning. It was about not giving up on her dreams.

> I may not have won a gold medal, but I won something far more important: my *dignity*.
>
> —**Yusra Mardini, UNHCR animation, 2017**

Yusra flies through the water in the women's 100-meter butterfly race.

Making Waves

During the Olympics, news about Team Refugee spread. People wanted to hear the athletes', inspiring stories. Yusra was interviewed by journalists from all over the world. The Games ended on August 21, but Yusra was just starting to make waves.

? THINK ABOUT IT

What do you think Yusra meant when she said she had won her dignity? Why do you think refugees might feel as though they do not have dignity?

Standing Together

After the Olympics, many people wanted to meet Yusra. She was invited to share her story with people all over the world, including many **politicians**. In September, she traveled to the United Nations in New York City. There she was invited to speak at the Leaders' Summit on Refugees. Yusra also received many awards and recognitions including the UNICEF Global Goal Awards Girl Award for her work creating progress for girls. With her sister Sarah, she was given a Bambi Award (German media prize) Silent Hero recognition. Yusra and her sister Sarah presented Pope Francis with an award at the Bambi Award ceremony.

Sarah and Yusra pose with their Bambi Awards at the awards ceremony in Berlin, Germany.

Sarah's Story

Yusra's sister Sarah has also shared her story to raise awareness about refugees. In 2016, she returned to the Greek island of Lesbos where she and Yusra had landed more than a year earlier. She works as a volunteer, using skills she learned as a lifeguard in Syria. She helps boats carrying refugees reach safety on shore. In Germany, she attends college and plans to study human rights.

> " *I will tell it [my story], until everyone has [learned] a lesson from it.*
>
> **— Yusra in an interview with TINCON Berlin, July 2017**

A Voice for Refugees

In April 2017, the UNHCR made Yusra a **goodwill ambassador**. Goodwill ambassadors are people who spread awareness about a cause. Yusra is the youngest person to ever receive this honor. In her work for the UNHCR, she shares positive messages and stories about her experiences and the refugee crisis. She often uses **social media** to spread her message.

The UNHCR

The United Nations (UN) is an organization that is made up of many countries. The UN High Commissioner for Refugees (UNHCR) helps people who have fled their homeland. It provides food, shelter, and helps refugees find new homes.

? THINK ABOUT IT

Social media allows a person to connect with people all over the world. How do you think this helps Yusra share her story?

Yusra Mardini
UNHCR's Goodwill Ambassador

As a goodwill ambassador, Yusra asks people to stand with her to support people escaping from conflict.

The Next Chapter

Yusra's story is so inspiring it is being made into a movie. She has written a book about her journey, called *Butterfly: From Refugee to Olympian—My Story of Rescue, Hope, and Triumph*. In the pool, Yusra is focused on training for the 2020 Olympics in Japan. Yusra has also become an ambassador for the sportswear company Under Armour. Down the road, she has said she would like to be a pilot or a swimming coach.

> " The main goal in my life is to represent refugees in a good way, to show everyone that refugees are people that can achieve like everyone in this world, and of course to win an Olympic medal, a gold. "
>
> — **Yusra Mardini, Facebook Live interview, 2017**

In addition to her school work and UNHCR duties, Yusra has ten training sessions a week.

Take a Stand

Yusra is using her voice to tell the world that refugees are ordinary people who live ordinary lives. In their home countries, they went to school, were educated, and raised families. They worked as teachers, doctors, and shopkeepers. Many, like Yusra, had dreams that were interrupted or ended. War and conflict destroyed their countries and they fled to survive.

#WithRefugees

Speaking at important world gatherings has given a new direction to the girl who swam for her life. In 2017, she gave a speech in front of world leaders at the World Economic Forum. Yusra asked them to stand up and fight the fear and hatred of refugees. Her words are reaching people. She supported the UNHCR #WithRefugees campaign. It included an online **petition** supporting refugees and presented to world leaders.

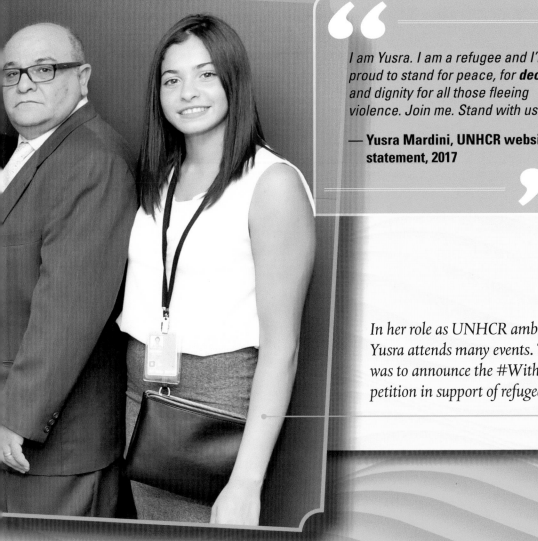

> 66
>
> *I am Yusra. I am a refugee and I'm proud to stand for peace, for **decency** and dignity for all those fleeing violence. Join me. Stand with us.*
>
> — **Yusra Mardini, UNHCR website statement, 2017**
>
> 99

In her role as UNHCR ambassador, Yusra attends many events. This event was to announce the #WithRefugees petition in support of refugees.

Writing Prompts

1. What challenges did Yusra overcome? What traits did she display? Use examples from the text to support your answer.

2. Do you think all countries should accept refugees? Why or why not?

3. How do stories such as Yusra's help raise awareness about the global refugee crisis?

Learning More

Books

My Beautiful Birds by Suzanne Del Rizzo. Pajama Press, 2017.

A Refugee's Journey from Syria by Helen Mason. Crabtree Publishing, 2017.

Syria by Julie Murray. ABDO Publishing, 2017.

Refugees and Migrants by Ceri Roberts. Barron's Educational Publishers, 2017.

Stepping Stones: A Refugee Family's Journey by Margriet Ruurs. Orca Book Publishers, 2016.

Websites

www.yusra-mardini.com
Visit Yusra's website to learn about her work with refugees and swimming career.

www.unhcr.org/yusra-mardini.html
Learn more about Yusra and her work as a goodwill ambassador for the UNHCR.

searchingforsyria.org/en/
Searching for Syria is an interactive website that presents pictures, statistics, and videos that help explain the war in Syria

www.un.org/en/events/peaceday/
The United Nations produced this animated video about Yusra's journey to increase awareness about World Refugee Day, which is celebrated on June 20.

www.unhcr.org/withrefugees/petition/
With an adult's permission, sign the #WithRefugees petition.

Glossary

Please note: Some bold-faced words are defined in the text

ambassador A person who represents something, such as a cause or a country

asylum Protection or shelter

borders Lines that separate one country or state from another

capsizing Turning over

civil war A war that is fought among people living in the same country

crisis A difficult, unstable time

decency Being polite, honest, and respectful toward others

democracy A political system in which people vote for their leaders

dignity Deserving respect

goodwill Kind and helpful feelings or attitude

heat In sports, a qualifying race in which the winner moves on to another event

illegally Not allowed by law

inspired Made people want to do something

judo A sport in which opponents try to throw or wrestle each other to the ground

legally Allowed by law

natural disaster An event, such as a hurricane or flood, that causes extensive damage

persecuted To be made to suffer because of a belief, such as a religion

petition A written request given by someone, usually supported by individual signatures

physiotherapist A person who treats an injury or illness through methods such as exercise and massage

politicians Elected people who are involved in the government

rebel A person or group who fights against a government or ruler

scholarship Money given to a person for their education

social media Forms of electronic communication, such as a website, that allow people to share information

traits Qualities that stand out about a person or a group of people

translator A person who changes written or spoken words from one language to another

Index

asylum 16
Bambi Award 24
boat capsizing 13
book 27
civil war 8, 9
Damascus 6, 10
Germany 10, 15, 16, 25
Greece 10, 11, 14–15, 25

Lesbos 14–15, 25
Mardini, Sarah 6, 13, 17, 25
Mardini family 7, 9
Olympics 4, 7, 20–21, 22–23, 27
refugee camps, 15
refugee crisis, 4, 11
refugees 4, 5, 9, 11, 10–11, 20, 26
Rio 2016 Olympics 4, 7, 20–21, 22–23

smugglers 11
sponsorships 27
swimming 6, 9, 10, 17, 18
Syria 4, 5, 6, 7, 8, 9, 10
Team Refugee 20–21
Turkey 9, 10–11, 12
UNICEF 24
UNHCR 26, 29